WHAT MATTERS?

Find Your Values,
Live Your Values,
Give Others Permission to do the Same

Coach on the Go

Anytime. Anywhere. Anything's Possible.

WHAT MATTERS?

Find Your Values,
Live Your Values,
Give Others Permission to do the Same

For volume discounts for your organization or learning community, please contact Danielle Reed directly at coachonthego@albertacom.com

Anytime. Anywhere. Anything's Possible.

WELCOME!

Years ago, finding my values was the key. I was living a life I no longer loved. I felt like I was on a hamster wheel. Waking up, racing through life, going to bed exhausted and hitting repeat. What I realized was that how I was living was not at all aligned with my values and what mattered. So I spent time figuring out what my key values were, I started to live them with intention each day and everything changed. I began to feel like myself. I began to wake up happy and excited for the day ahead. I began to go to sleep with a smile on my face. I began to say yes to the things that aligned and no to the things that didn't. It seemed too simple. I was waiting for life to go back to the way it was. It never happened. Here I am almost six years later and I can tell you that finding my values and choosing to intentionally live them changed my life! I hope that you will have your own amazing AHA moments as you uncover and live your values.

My Top Values are:
Authenticity
Balance
Connection
Gratitude
Humor
Health
Learning
Legacy
Optimism
Organization
Understanding

What are values?

Please finish the following statements:

I grew up believing values were...

_____

I think some of my key values are...

_____

Other thoughts or reflections about values?

Values are...

Your values are like an internal compass. They lead you to be who you want to be and to live the life you truly want. When you follow your compass, you tend to end your days feeling happy and fulfilled. When you don't follow your compass, your days tend to end in frustration, sadness, disconnection and exhaustion.

In fact, the best hint that you are off track with your values is that pit in the stomach feeling. When you notice you are feeling "off", stop and get curious. "What's going on for me right now?" The answer usually has something to do with being misaligned with your values and what matters.

I like to use the word PATH to refer to the place where you "want" to be. The path is where your values lie. It is the place that you can come back to any time. It's what matters most to you.

I use the word ACT to refer to the place where you don't want to be. It doesn't feel good. When you are in the act, you are likely trying to "fit in", be someone you aren't and you sacrifice your values to stay there.

When you are on your PATH, you feel happy, you feel authentic and you have friends in your life who know exactly who you are.

When you are in the ACT, you feel unhappy, inauthentic and you tend to have friends in your life who like things about you that aren't even the real you. These friendships don't tend to last very long.

REFLECTION:

Where are you right now? Are you aligned with who you want to be? Are you on the PATH or in the ACT? Be honest with yourself. It's okay if you are in the ACT. We've all been there. This workbook is going to help you move back toward the PATH.

Trust the process.

Values are...

The GAP

The gap is the space between who you want to be and who you are actually showing up as. The smaller the gap, the more content you feel. The larger the gap, the more disconnected and lost you may feel.

The goal is not to be perfect and show up 100% aligned every day. That would be unrealistic....we are human. The goal is to spend more days aligned with what matters than not.

The gap between who we want to be and who we are actually being is the place where anxiety, depression, lack of fulfillment and "blah" happens.

Your internal compass knows who you want to be and how you want to live your life. You just need to find the courage to follow it!

Let me tell you a story...
I was working in a school one day and I met a student who seemed very unhappy. She was quiet, kept to herself and when others spoke she said mean things back to them. She found herself in the principal's office almost daily. She looked at me like she hated me. One day I asked her if she would come meet with me. Reluctantly, she agreed. We sat down and I asked her questions to try to find out what her top 10 value words were. It took her a while, but she handed the sheet back to me with her top 10 values on it, and I asked her, "Which value is easiest for you to live each day?" Her response was, "None of them!"

My heart ached. But she was being honest, she rarely lived her values. Some of her value words were: family, belonging, achievement, friendship, safety, health & honesty. Can you imagine if these are what you wanted in your life and yet each day you woke up and they weren't present? Living in the act is hard. None of us want to be there. Yet we find ourselves there at different stages in our lives. The key is to begin to close the gap. Find one value that you can begin to live and go from there.

Why 5-10 Values?

If you have 40 top values, it is hard to wake up and live your life with intention. For me, when I wake up, I plant my feet on the ground and before I begin my day, I say my top 10 values aloud. As I say each one I make the intention to truly live it.
When my day ends, I head to bed and before I fall asleep, I say my values aloud again and I do a check in. Did I live this value today? How did it show up? How did it feel to live it?
Were there values that I didn't live today? If so, why not?
Did I kick values under the carpet myself? Did others around me stomp on my values? What is my intention for tomorrow?

If you had 40 values, it would make it very difficult to live with intention. Your top 10 are the ones that matter most. The values that if you couldn't be, do or have...you'd be devastated!
For me, humor is a huge part of my life. If you told me I could no longer have humor each day, it would feel so empty.
That's how I know that humor is a value.

As well, sometimes we want to only pick values that we are currently living and steer away from those we want but feel are impossible to achieve. You MUST choose the values you most want to live even if they seem like a stretch.
For years, I desperately wanted balance. It was a value for me. However, I thought it was impossible. "I will never have balance!" Believing that I would never have it meant that I would always have a gap between what I wanted and who I was. That meant that I would often go to bed with a pit in the stomach feeling. Your values must be what matters most...even if they feel far away right now.

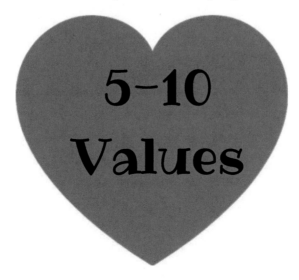

Why do Values Matter? The Research

,Here are some key pieces of research that made me determined to begin to live my own life by my values and give others permission to do the same:

Search Institute

For many years, I brought the work of the Search Institute into the schools I worked in. At Search, they share the top 8 asset categories that youth need in order to live successful, happy lives. One of the 8 categories is that youth have positive values.

Brené Brown

When I first heard Brené Brown speak, she said, "There is only one thing we must carry in our back pockets with us at all times....a very clear sense of our values."

Roots of Empathy - Dr.Marilyn Price-Mitchell

Dr. Price-Mitchell's research shows that one of the top 3 common sources of positive youth development is, "Positive Values - Children who grow
to be engaged, successful adults have and live positive values from a young age."
She also shares the top 5 qualities that youth look for in a role model -
#2 says, "Youth look for role models who know and live their values in the world."

Mental Strength - Amy Morin

Amy Morin, psychotherapist, says, "Developing mental strength is about finding the courage to live according to your values."

Shefali Tsabary

In her book, The Conscious Parent, Shefali Tsabary talks a lot about seeing our kids in their "as is" state. She says, "The ability to see - really see - our children separate from who we are is our greatest gift to them." We can really see our kids when we know what matters to them - when we help them find and live their own values.

Dr. Larry Berkelhammer

Dr.Berkelhammer, a mind body medicine psychologist, says, "A life value cannot be achieved; it can only be lived. It is a way of being or a human quality you value. These ways of being and qualities are golden; when you identify them and then consciously engage in the mindfulness practice of living in harmony with them, you tap into a wellspring of health and happiness—this is what is meant by life mastery. The mere act of focusing on what you value can shift your entire experience of life."

A Story...

Let me tell you another story....

When my oldest son was born, I assumed that he would be just like me. I gave birth to him so it made sense right?

I was athletic and competitive as a youth. I played volleyball, basketball, soccer, tennis, badminton, and I played them well. I assumed he would too!

When Nolan was born, my first instinct was to sign him up for hockey. We live in Alberta, Canada....so hockey just seemed like a no brainer. Of course he is going to love sports...he's my kid!

I remember one of the first games he played as a goalie in his Atom year. He got into the car after the game and I immediately asked him if he wanted to do extra goalie training sessions or a goalie camp.

His response was, "I'm hungry. Can we go to A&W?"

I tried to talk hockey but he stayed set on getting a hamburger.

Later that day, my husband and I got talking and he asked why I thought Nolan should do these camps and extra sessions. It stopped me in my tracks.

I thought he should because THAT'S WHAT I WOULD HAVE DONE.

I was trying to make him like me rather than see him for who he was.

I was trying to pull him onto MY path, rather than give him permission to choose his own path. WOW!

I had no idea I was doing that. My unconscious self was saying, "Listen, I'm awesome and if you are like me, you'll be awesome too!" lol

When he was nine years old, I did his values with him and what I discovered was that he was like me in some ways, but very different in other ways.

He did not have any values that had to do with athletics or competitiveness.

OMG...he was NOT me!

But what he did have was responsibility, inclusion, leadership, courage...

He was happiest when he was at his leadership option, when he was volunteering at the JET summer camp with young kids, being part of youth council, and when he helped in the grade one classroom.

If I had continued to try to make him like me, I would have missed the best part about who he is and what matters to him.

It's so important to notice when you are trying to pull others onto your path rather than giving them permission to choose their own path and follow their own inner compass.

How do I find my Values?

I am going to share with you three ways you can find your values. You can choose whichever one works for you....or maybe you will try all three and create your list from that.

STEP #1: Amazing Day

Days feel amazing when you choose to live aligned with your values.

In the space below, list all the things that are involved in an amazing day for you.

What would you do?

How would you spend your time?

Who would you be?

Create your list and then pull your values from it.

HERE'S AN EXAMPLE:

Amazing Day	Value(s)
Workout at the gym	Health
Breakfast with my kids	Connection, humor, balance
Dinner put in the crockpot	Organization
Work on my course	Learning
Workshop for adults/youth	Connection, authenticity, gratitude, humor, optimism

Your turn:

Amazing Day	Value(s)

TIP:
Try to avoid grabbing a list of values from the Internet and selecting your values from it. Your ego will take over and tell you what you "should" pick. Choosing values from your current, lived experiences will give you the most honest, accurate list of your values.

How do I find my values?

STEP #2: Things that frustrate me or make me angry

You feel frustrated when what you value is not being honored either by yourself or by those around you.

In the space below, list all the things that frustrate or make you angry.

The flip of what makes you frustrated or angry is a value that is being stomped on.

Find the flip of the things that frustrate or make you angry.

EXAMPLE:

Frustration(s)	**Flip - Value(s) being stomped on**
I don't want this....	*I want this...*
Gossiping	loyalty, integrity, honesty, trust
Being too busy	balance
People who litter	nature, environment, respect
Failing / Not doing well	achievement, accomplishment, success
Being left out	acceptance, belonging, inclusion, fairness, connection

Your turn:

Frustrations   **Flip - Value(s)**

TIP:
Do NOT list people.
Try to list situations that make you frustrated or angry. Your boss at work may make you angry, but it's what he/she does that actually makes you mad. Maybe he/she is a micromanager. Your value may be respect, trust or competency.
Get specific.

How do I find my values?

What values do you have so far from the above exercises?
It doesn't matter if it's 2 or 100...just write them down

*Write them all over this page. HAVE FUN! Maybe use colored pens or pencil crayons. Write them in a list or make a word puzzle with them. Do whatever feels right for you.

How many words are on your page so far? _____

TIP:
At the beginning, just write down whatever words resonate with you without thinking too much about it. Later in the process you will begin to shorten your list.
For now, just notice which words tug on your heart. Put them on the list.

How do I find my values?

OPTIONAL ACTIVITY: WHAT MATTERS™ Values cards

If you have the What Matters™ Values cards, you can also do the following activity:

Open up your values cards

Read through the cards one at a time

Make a YES pile and a NO pile

The YES pile are those that resonate. You want to do/have/be that on a daily basis. You are happiest when you are.

The NO pile are the ones that don't resonate.

Once you have your YES pile, begin to group ones that are similar. For example: kindness, compassion, caring are all related. Try to choose one word to represent that grouping. Choose the word that you like the best.

As you go through all 85 cards and answer the questions at the bottom of each card, you will get very clear about what your top values are.

To order the What Matters™cards: www.coachonthego.net/shop

TIP:
Always choose your own values. Avoid asking others to tell you what they think your values are. Trust your own heart. Sometimes people see behaviors in us that we do because we think we have to, but we don't always value them. Only you know what truly matters to YOU!

Now what?

Take your list of values from:
Your AMAZING DAY
Things that Frustrate or Make you Angry
What Matters™ cards

Take as much time as you need to get your list down to your top 10 words:

1. _____

2. _____

3. _____

4. _____

5. _____

6. _____

7. _____

8. _____

9. _____

10. _____

TIP:
There is no timeline for getting this done. For some people, it happens quickly. For others, it takes a while. Give yourself permission for it to happen when it happens. If you rush it, you may miss words or pick the wrong words. You want words that resonate for YOU!

How aligned are you?

Write your top 10 values here:

Which value is easiest for you to live each day?

Explain _____

Which value is the most challenging for you to live each day?

Explain _____

TIP:
Do not judge yourself
if your values are not being
lived or honored right now.
It happens.
Instead, get excited about the
possibilities ahead as you begin to
live your values with greater
intention.

Keep them Visible

If you want to:

- Live your values with intention
- Set out on your day with your values in mind
- Course correct when you find yourself in the act

Then you have to:

- Know your value words

How can you keep them in your mind:

1. Have them as your screen saver on your phone.
2. Make a values fan to hang somewhere that you will see them each day.
   On the mirror where you brush your teeth, on your night table....etc.
3. Create a WORDLE
4. Make a values wall or framed picture of your value words

Other ideas?

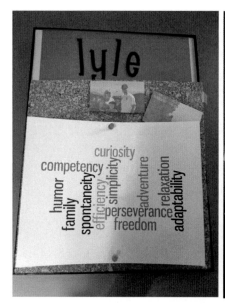  

Set an Intention & Reflect

If you want to live your values with intention, you have to begin your day with them in mind and you have to reflect and assess at the end of the day. Your intention is what you want to focus on or make happen in that day. Your reflection is your assessment of how the day went.
Try for 10 days to set an intention and do a nightly reflection.

Example:

Intention: Today I will get my workspace more organized. It's been bothering me lately. Organization is something I value.
Reflection: I ended my day happy. All values felt really aligned today.

Your turn:

	INTENTION	REFLECTION
Day 1:		
Day 2:		
Day 3:		
Day 4:		
Day 5:		
Day 6:		
Day 7:		
Day 8:		
Day 9:		
Day 10:		

What did you notice after 10 days?

What Happens when Values conflict ?

Sometimes your values will conflict with another person's values. It may feel like a win/lose situation. One person gets to have their value honored (win) and one person doesn't (lose). But that's not how it works. Let me tell you a story to illustrate this point.

My boys came home from school one day, and I could hear them bickering all the way from the bus to the house. When they came in the front door I asked them what all the arguing was about. My youngest son said, "I want to go outside and play baseball and Nolan wants to sit in the house and watch TV. How can I play baseball by myself?" Now that is a legitimate question, but I told the boys to go over to the value wall and look at each other's values and see if they could figure out what the issue was. Less than a minute later Spencer said, "I know what it is. I have being active as one of my top values and Nolan has solitude/relaxation as one of his." (insert AHA moment here)

So my next question to them was, "How can you both have your values honored?"

You see....I believe one of the reasons we have so much conflict in our world is that we sometimes forget to take our eyes off of our own path to see what matters to other people. We think that we need to live our value and that's all that matters. I can tell you...only focusing on having your values honored is not who any of us want to be.

So I asked the boys, "How do you think you can both have your values honored?"

Spencer said, "Nolan, how long do you want to sit on the couch and watch TV?"

Nolan answered, "I want to watch this one show."

Spencer asked, "Then will you play baseball with me after?"

Nolan replied, "Yes."

WOW...that was easy! We often have conversations like this when there are conflicts, and we always find a way to resolve them that honors both people's values. It's not hard. You just have to be willing to focus on what matters to you as well as what matters to those around you.

What Happens when Values conflict - Story #2...

Adults are no different...we also have conflicts with values.
Let me share another example:

One of my top values is ORGANIZATION. One of my husband's values is SPONTANEITY. Are you already feeling the pain?

One day on a beautiful Friday afternoon, my husband called from work and said, "We should go camping! It's supposed to be such a beautiful weekend!"

My immediate response was, "You mean this weekend? Like today?"

And truly, I was thinking, "Not a chance. We don't have groceries. None of the bikes are packed. The trailer needs to be cleaned. You are nuts to think this is going to work."

My husband on the other hand was so enthusiastic about it, telling me how we could make it work.

Now...I stopped to think about which values were colliding and here's what I realized. We were both trying to live a value. Organization for me, spontaneity for him. Neither one of us was right or wrong. Neither one of us was the good guy or the bad guy. We just were going with the pull of our compasses.

If I put my foot down and said it can't happen...only my value would be honored and his would be stomped on. That's not who I want to be.

If he said, "I have 12 hotdogs and 12 buns, let's go," only his value would be honored and mine would be stomped on. That's not who he wants to be.

I had to ask for what I needed and it sounded something like this, "You know how important organization is for me. Going camping with no notice stresses me out. But I also know that spontaneity is important for you, so let's see if we can figure this out."

His response was, "Tell the boys to load the bikes, you text me a grocery list that I can grab after work, and you clean the trailer. We could leave around supper time."

I breathed a sigh of relief. Now this worked for me!

We both got our values honored and it didn't take a fight to get there. It just took me saying, "I get you. I get what matters to you. I see you. Please do the same for me." And luckily, he did the same.

How can you begin to live your values and give others permission to do the same?

Seeing Others Through a Values Lens

It's time to move from **YOU** to **OTHERS**. It's time to see how you can change **JUDGMENT** for **CURIOSITY** and **COMPASSION** by using a Values lens. Here's how I think about judgment:

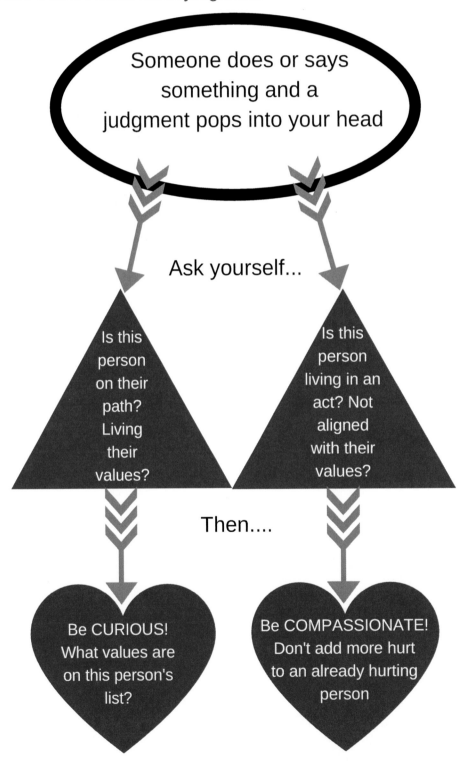

Someone does or says something and a judgment pops into your head

Ask yourself...

Is this person on their path? Living their values?

Is this person living in an act? Not aligned with their values?

Then....

Be CURIOUS! What values are on this person's list?

Be COMPASSIONATE! Don't add more hurt to an already hurting person

Seeing Others Through a Values Lens

Let me give you some real life situations to show you how this looks...

For young kids:
You go outside for recess at school. You want to play soccer. You go to the soccer field and one student is holding the ball, telling each person what team they are on, making all the rules and being the referee.

Your judgment: You are so bossy! You always tell us what to do.

Ask yourself: Is this person on their path or in an act? (They are on their path)

BE CURIOUS! What values are likely on this kid's value list?

leadership, organization, order, rules...

They aren't a bad person. They just have different values than you.

For teenagers
A classmate is hanging around your group of friends at break time. He/she is asking questions and saying things that sound a little awkward. He/she is trying to be funny.

Your judgment: Why are you here? Quit bugging us. Go find some friends.

Ask yourself: Is this person on their path or in an act? (They are on their path)

BE CURIOUS! What values are likely on this kid's value list?

belonging, connection, friendship, recognition, acceptance, humor...

They aren't trying to be annoying. They are trying to live their values.

OR

A peer in your school is dressing inappropriately, talking about parties and troubling situations that she has been involved with.

Your judgment: What a _____! She thinks she is so cool!

Ask yourself: Is this person on their path or in an act? (They are in an act)

Be COMPASSIONATE! When you are living in an act...it's hard! You don't have to agree with the person's behavior, but if you can recognize that they are hurting, you don't feel the need to add more hurt to their life. Feel with them. Imagine what it would be like if that was you.

For adults
A parent at the local hockey arena is in the stands yelling non-stop during the game.

Your judgment: What a crazy parent! He/she is out of control. Get a grip!

Ask yourself: Is this person on their path or in an act?

If the yelling is not hurtful, it's likely that this parent is on their path.

BE CURIOUS! What values are likely on this person's value list?

success, achievement, enthusiasm, accomplishment, competitiveness...

HOWEVER...

If the yelling is negative towards the kids and referees, it is likely this parent is in an act.

BE COMPASSIONATE! When you are living in an act...it's hard! You don't have to agree with the person's behavior, but if you can recognize that they are hurting, you don't feel the need to add more hurt to their life. Feel with them. Imagine what it would be like if that was you.

Seeing Others Through a Values Lens

Your turn...
Think of scenarios in your life where you noticed judgment pop into your mind. Describe the scenario and then go through the steps.

Scenario:

Path or Act? _____

If path - BE CURIOUS - What values matter to this person?

If act - BE COMPASSIONATE - What can you do?

Do this when you notice yourself judging. Do your eyes soften when you look at others through a values lens? Do you notice your heart feels kinder?

What else do you notice?

Seeing Others Through a Values Lens

When we choose curiosity, we open our MINDS to:

1. Seeing people as unique beings.
2. Embracing differences.
3. Learning to respect, appreciate and accept others for who they are.
4. Giving others permission to live on their own path.

When we choose compassion, we open our HEARTS to:

1. Allow for imperfection.
2. Generosity - believing people are doing the best they can in that moment.
3. Struggle in others
4. Common Humanity - It could be you!
5. Stop adding more hurt to an already hurting person.
6. Staying authentic and aligned with who you want to be!

Seeing Others Through a Values Lens

For one week, I want you to commit to daily reflection about judgment, curiosity and compassion.

Scenario
What happened?

Judgment
What thought popped into your mind?

Curiosity or Compassion
Did this person need curiosity or compassion? Explain.

How did it feel?

Making Values a Habit

To make values a habit, you have to work at it...

Start each day with intention

Read or say your values aloud

Set an intention

During the day, notice when your mood shifts and reconnect with your values. Is one being stomped on? Are you out of alignment? If so, what do you need to do to shift a bad moment back to a great day?

At the end of the day reflect...

What value(s) did I honor today? How?

What value(s) were challenging to live? Why?

How can I be more intentional tomorrow?

Did I have judgments pop into my mind today? What did I do with them?

This is our kitchen wall. It makes for great dinner conversations!

Reflection

What are your key learnings after completing this workbook? Write them all down. Read them through and set your intention for the days to come.

My intention is:

Notes

Notes

Appendix: Values List

Acceptance
Accountability
Achievement
Adaptability
Adventure
Altruism
Ambition
Authenticity
Balance
Beauty
Belonging
Caring
Challenge
Collaboration
Commitment
Compassion
Competency
Competitiveness
Confidence
Connection
Contentment
Contribution
Cooperation
Courage
Creativity
Curiosity
Dignity
Diversity
Efficiency
Encouragement
Enthusiasm
Equality
Ethics
Excellence
Fairness
Faith
Family
Financial stability
Forgiveness
Freedom
Generosity
Gratitude

Health
Helpfulness
Home
Honesty
Hope
Humor
Imagination
Inclusion
Integrity
Intelligence
Kindness
Leadership
Learning
Love
Loyalty
Nature
Optimism
Organization
Patience
Peace
Perseverance
Pride
Recognition
Reflection
Relaxation
Reliability
Respect
Responsibility
Safety
Service
Silence
Silliness
Simplicity
Spirituality
Success
Time
Trust
Truth
Understanding
Uniqueness
Usefulness
Wealth
Wisdom

For more information...

To order What Matters™ Values cards or to watch videos on how to use the cards:

www.coachonthego.net/shop

Look for:
30 Days to What Matters - A Values Journal
on Amazon.com

For more information, follow me on

Facebook: www.facebook.com/coachonthego.net

Twitter: @coachonthego_a

Instagram: coach_onthego

Thank you for choosing values, curiosity and compassion!
With gratitude,
Danielle Reed

Coach
on the Go
Anytime. Anywhere. Anything's Possible.

Manufactured by Amazon.ca
Bolton, ON